3 4028 07933 6302
HARRIS COUNTY PUBLIC LIBRARY

J B Nanak
Singh, Rina
Guru Nanak : the first Sikh
guru

$24.95
ocn697261496
02/29/2012

W9-DGU-509

GURU NANAK
THE FIRST SIKH GURU

RINA SINGH

ILLUSTRATED BY

ANDRÉE POULIOT

GROUNDWOOD BOOKS / HOUSE OF ANANSI PRESS

TORONTO   BERKELEY

Text copyright © 2011 by Rina Singh
Illustrations copyright © 2011 by Andrée Pouliot
Published in Canada and the USA in 2011 by Groundwood Books

All rights reserved. No part of this publication may be reproduced, stored in a retrieval system or transmitted, in any form or by any means, without the prior written consent of the publisher or a license from The Canadian Copyright Licensing Agency (Access Copyright). For an Access Copyright license, visit www.accesscopyright.ca or call toll free to 1-800-893-5777

Groundwood Books / House of Anansi Press
110 Spadina Avenue, Suite 801, Toronto, Ontario M5V 2K4
or c/o Publishers Group West
1700 Fourth Street, Berkeley, CA 94710

We acknowledge for their financial support of our publishing program the Canada Council for the Arts, the Government of Canada through the Canada Book Fund (CBF) and the Ontario Arts Council.

 Canada Council
for the Arts
Conseil des Arts
du Canada

 ONTARIO ARTS COUNCIL
CONSEIL DES ARTS DE L'ONTARIO

Library and Archives Canada Cataloguing in Publication
Singh, Rina
Guru Nanak : the first Sikh Guru / Rina Singh ; Andrée Pouliot,
illustrator.
ISBN 978-0-88899-958-0
1. Nanak, Guru, 1469-1539—Juvenile literature. 2. Sikh gurus—
India—Biography—Juvenile literature. I. Pouliot, Andrée
II. Title.
BL2017.85.N36S55 2011   j294.6092   C2011-900511-5

The miniature paintings were done in gouache and watercolor pencil on Strathmore Bristol card.
Design by Michael Solomon
Printed and bound in Hongkong

TABLE OF CONTENTS

Introduction 9

Nanak's Birth 12

Childhood 15

Growing Up 20

Sultanpur 25

Enlightenment 28

Nanak's Travels 32

The First Journey 35

The Second Journey 42

The Third Journey 46

The Fourth Journey 49

Kartarpur 55

Nanak's Death 57

Map 60

The Sikh Gurus 61

Glossary 62

For Further Reading 64

For Angad. — RS

For my mother, Sarah, who called me to India. — AP

INTRODUCTION

G URU NANAK, the founder of the Sikh religion, was a gentle teacher, a social reformer, a mystic and an amazing poet. To appreciate his teachings, it's helpful to understand what it was like in India during the 1400s.

India was occupied by people of two different faiths — Hinduism and Islam. Hindus were natives of India who believed in hundreds of gods and goddesses and practiced the caste system. The system was like a ladder with four rungs. Brahmins (priests) were at the top; Kshatriyas (rulers, warriors and landowners) were second; Vaishyas (merchants) were next; and Shudras (untouchables) were at the bottom.

The followers of Islam, on the other hand, were Arab Muslims who had been trading with India for centuries and had begun to settle there. They believed in the teachings of the prophet Muhammad. Islam spread peacefully and both religions lived in relative harmony, till Turkish invaders, led by Timur in 1398, plundered the country. The Turks forced Hindus to convert to Islam, increasing religious tensions in India.

Nanak was born when the two religions had turned against each other and, in his own words, the times had become like a dagger:

Kings have become butchers.
In the darkness of the evil night
goodness has fled and the moon of truth
is nowhere to be found.

In Nanak's poetry lay the seeds of a new faith that drew on traditions from Hindu (Bhakti) and Islamic (Sufi) beliefs. His search for truth led him to a religion that embraced all humanity. People who followed him began calling him "guru," which means teacher, and they called themselves "Sikhs," which means disciples.

Nanak's teachings sum up the basic beliefs of the Sikh faith: Worship one God, treat everyone equally, work honestly, share with the less fortunate and serve the community. He founded a religion that was based on ethics, social responsibility and social justice. He shocked Indian society by giving women equal status:

From a woman, man is born;
to a woman he is married.
From women, kings are born.
Then why call her evil?
Without women there would be no one at all.

He was way ahead of his times because even now, more than five hundred years later, women are still struggling for respect in many parts of the world.

The Sikh faith evolved with the nine gurus who followed Guru Nanak. Guru Gobind Singh, the tenth guru, had to resort to the sword to protect the young Sikh nation from the tyranny of Aurangzeb, the last Mughal emperor. He gave military organization to the Sikhs and established a baptism that would set them apart from people of other faiths. He also made it compulsory for baptized Sikhs to wear the five Ks — *kes* (uncut hair to give them a distinct identity), *kangha* (a wooden comb to keep the hair tidy), *kara* (a steel or iron bangle as a reminder to do good deeds), *kaccha* (a long undergarment to show self control) and *kirpan* (a small sword to remind Sikhs not to be bystanders when people are treated unjustly).

He declared the mission of Guru Nanak complete and said that the Sikh holy book, the *Guru Granth Sahib*, would now rule the Sikhs. It has 1430 pages of poetry written by the Sikh gurus and includes verses of Hindu saints and Muslim mystics as well. Every *gurdwara* (Sikh place of worship) has a copy of the holy book.

Guru Nanak lived during a time that is well remembered by history — when Babur, the first of the Mughal emperors, invaded India; Christopher Columbus discovered America; Vasco Da Gama found India; and Ferdinand Magellan sailed from Spain, becoming the first person to voyage around the world. Yet exact details of Nanak's life are unknown.

What we do know comes from four different sources, all of them versions of *Janam sakhis* (birth stories), that were written in Punjabi by faithful disciples. The stories may have been embellished with metaphors and miracles, resulting in accounts of Guru Nanak's life that are told in the language of myth and history. Sikhs do not try to explain the miracles but fondly read about their guru's life to understand his teachings. I hope the reader will do the same to understand the beliefs of an exceptional poet and a remarkable guru, who was divinely inspired and whose teachings come to us in his own words.

NANAK'S BIRTH

THE STORY OF NANAK, the first guru of the Sikhs, began more than five hundred years ago in Talwandi, a village not far from Lahore. Talwandi was at the edge of a forest that lay between two rivers. As far as the eye could see there was a wasteland of sand dotted with small shrubs and patches of green fields. The village itself was a maze of dusty, narrow lanes, lined with low-roofed houses.

It was a place of extreme weather. The frosty winters were followed by brief springs, when the desert shrubs burst into flower, filling the air with fragrance. After the long, sweltering summers came the monsoons. The rains drenched the parched earth, making the grass dense, bringing out insects, serpents, birds and beasts that filled the air with sounds.

In the early hours of April 15, 1469, Kalu Bedi, a Hindu tax official, paced outside his house awaiting the birth of his second child. Inside, his wife, Tripta, was in labor.

As soon as the baby was born, a light flashed through the room, dazzling the Muslim midwife. She had never witnessed such a birth, for instead of crying as he took his first breath, the baby laughed gently like a saint.

Kalu eagerly summoned the village priest to draw a horoscope for his son.

Tears welled up in the priest's eyes as he held the baby.

"What do you see?" asked Kalu, alarmed. "Is something wrong?"

"I foresee that your son will grow up to be a great teacher, and I will not live to see his glory," said the priest.

He returned thirteen days later, as was the custom, and named the newborn Nanak after his sister, Nanaki. And thus began an extraordinary life.

CHILDHOOD

AS A CHILD, Nanak shared his sweets and toys with the other village children, which endeared him to his mother and sister. His father, however, thought that he was wasteful.

When Nanak was seven years old, he was sent to the Hindu priest-scholar who ran the village school. The teacher held his classes under the trees where students, seated in neat rows on mats, repeated their lessons loudly. Nanak soon mastered the alphabet and amazed his teacher by writing a poem praising God on his wooden tablet.

But Kalu wanted his son to learn how to do math and accounting. When the teacher made an attempt to teach him numbers, Nanak said,

Burn worldly attachments and grind them into ink;
render your intellect onto paper.
Let God be the pen, awareness your scribe.
Write what the guru instructs.
Praise his name.
Write over and over again:
he is limitless, fathomless.

The teacher suggested that Nanak learn Sanskrit, the

language of the Hindu scriptures, even though it was usually reserved for Brahmins. Kalu agreed, determined for his son to move ahead in the world.

At the age of nine, Nanak began to spend time alone, daydreaming and roaming the fields and forests near the village. He would often stop wandering Hindu and Muslim holy men and have conversations with them. This worried Kalu, who wanted Nanak to prepare himself for a suitable occupation. He sought advice from his Muslim landlord, Rai Bular. At his suggestion, Kalu hired a Muslim priest-scholar to teach Persian and Arabic to Nanak. In just two years, Nanak was able to read the scriptures.

Around this time Nanak befriended a boy named Marjana. Marjana was a few years older and the only son of a Muslim couple from the Mirasi tribe of musicians and drummers. His mother, who had lost six children before him, named him Marjana (the one who will die) out of sheer despair. Every morning the family went from door-to-door singing and collecting alms. Fascinated by their music, Nanak urged Marjana to play the rebec and began to call him Mardana (the one who will not die).

When Nanak turned eleven, it was time for him to get the *janeu*, the sacred thread. A priest would place white cotton thread around his neck and over his shoulder to show that he was now a man. The thread also set apart the boys of the three upper castes from lower-caste boys. It was an important landmark in a young Hindu's life.

As was the custom, Kalu invited all their relatives, friends and neighbors for the *janeu* ceremony, which was to be followed by a grand feast. The servants washed the courtyard and built a mud platform especially for the occasion.

On the day of the ceremony, the priest drew sacred

diagrams on the ground with colored flour, lit incense and chanted mantras to purify the thread. Amidst the chanting, Nanak was invited to sit on the platform. But when the priest began to put the thread around his neck, Nanak stopped him.

"What is the purpose of this thread?" he asked.

The priest explained that the thread would initiate him into manhood and keep his heart pure.

"What if I choose to rob and cheat after I wear the thread? Will my heart still be pure?" asked Nanak.

The people looked on in shock. No one had ever questioned the rituals of their ancestors.

The priest made one last attempt. "Be an obedient son, Nanak, and wear the thread, or everyone will be greatly disappointed."

Nanak replied,

Make cotton out of mercy, thread out of contentment;
knot it with modesty and twist it with truth.
If you have such a thread, then put it on me,
a thread that never breaks or soils,
never burns or perishes.
Blessed are the ones, O Nanak,
who wear such a thread.

The priest walked away, and soon afterwards the assembly of people dissolved.

Kalu was devastated. He was convinced that his son was either possessed by an evil spirit or had gone utterly mad. He summoned a Muslim healer who tied an amulet to Nanak's arm and prepared to cast out the evil spirit. But Nanak just chided him for writing God's name on pieces of paper and selling them.

Then Kalu summoned a Hindu healer who felt Nanak's pulse. Nanak told him that the trouble was not in his body but in his soul. The healer declared that nothing was wrong with him.

GROWING UP

ONLY THE LANDLORD, Rai Bular, and Nanaki understood Nanak. Nanaki was not only Nanak's older sister but his friend too. She recognized her brother's holiness and protected him from their father's temper. Her marriage, arranged to Jairam of Sultanpur, was a turning point in Nanak's life. After she moved away, he grew more and more silent.

Distressed by his silence, Kalu came up with an idea. Since Nanak was happy in the fields and woods, he would ask his son to take the buffaloes for grazing. Nanak was delighted with the arrangement. It gave him time to wander undisturbed and to compose poetry praising God.

One day, as Nanak lay under a tree, the buffaloes he was supposed to be supervising strayed into a neighbor's field. When the neighbor saw the buffaloes eating his wheat, he went straight to Kalu and Rai Bular to complain. Rai Bular ordered his men to investigate the incident. But when they inspected the fields, the men found nothing wrong. They came back to report that the neighbor was lying. When the neighbor saw that not a blade of wheat had been touched, he fell to the ground saying that truly a miracle had happened.

On two other occasions, Rai Bular himself witnessed something strange. One evening, when he was returning

from inspecting his fields, he saw Nanak sleeping under a tree. What astonished him was that the shadows of all the trees had moved with the sun, except the one under which Nanak slept. It continued to shade him from the scorching rays. And on another occasion, he saw a deadly cobra spread its hood to shade Nanak as he slept.

Kalu, on the other hand, continued to be frustrated with Nanak's lack of interest in worldly affairs and constantly scolded him. When he suggested that Nanak could till the fields, his son replied,

> *Make your body the field,*
> *your mind the harvester.*
> *Sow the seeds of goodness.*
> *Let modesty be the water.*
> *Irrigate it with God's name.*
> *The seeds will then sprout*
> *and you can watch your home prosper.*

"Would you like to open a shop, then?" asked his exasperated father. And Nanak broke into song:

> *Make this ever dying body your shop.*
> *Stock the warehouse of contemplation*
> *with the merchandise of his true name.*
> *Good deeds will pay for the traveling expenses.*
> *You shall bring your profits home*
> *when you arrive in the land of the formless one.*

Kalu's frustration knew no bounds. Maybe trading would suit his son's restless temperament. So he made one more attempt. Kalu gave Nanak twenty silver rupees and asked him to go to the neighboring town and buy salt, sugar and spices at wholesale prices, which he could then sell for a profit.

"Invest wisely," he advised his son. He sent Bala, a Hindu man, to accompany him, since this was Nanak's first trading trip.

On their way to the town, Nanak and Bala passed through a forest where they saw a gathering of Hindu holy men in meditation. Some were standing in water, their eyes closed; some sat cross-legged, deep in prayer; some rested under trees, reading holy texts; and some stood with their hands joined, facing the sun.

Nanak was fascinated and stopped to make conversation with them. Bala began to feel uneasy. Nanak should be on his way to finish the task his father had set him, not stopping to talk to a bunch of holy men, he thought. But he couldn't convince Nanak to leave.

Nanak discovered that the holy men had not eaten for many days. He offered them the twenty rupees, but they refused, saying that money was of no use to them. They had no utensils and so couldn't cook food. They depended on the kindness of strangers.

In spite of Bala's protests, Nanak went to the town and bought rice, lentils, salt, sugar, fuel, pots and pans. He hurried back to cook a meal for the holy men, who showered him with blessings.

Nanak knew his father's temper, so when they returned home he decided to stay on the outskirts of their village. Bala went and broke the news to Kalu, who took a stick and went looking for his son. Bala then ran to Rai Bular, who rushed to the spot to defend Nanak.

"Where are the twenty rupees?" Kalu asked Nanak again and again.

"You unhappy man, you shout at Nanak for the sake of twenty rupees!" Rai Bular scolded him.

"I traded the twenty rupees for a blessing, and I thought it was a good bargain," said Nanak.

Rai Bular told Kalu not to treat Nanak like an ordinary person. But Kalu despaired at his son's aimlessness.

SULTANPUR

Nanaki's husband, Jairam, was a kind man who had taken a liking to Nanak. He felt that Kalu misunderstood his son, and that Nanak should move to Sultanpur and stay with them. He would help him find work. Kalu agreed to the plan, hoping the change would do his son good.

Jairam set up an appointment with the governor of Sultanpur, who was impressed with Nanak and appointed him storekeeper of his granary. This was an important job because taxes and salaries in those days were paid partly with grains and other provisions.

Nanak devoted himself to the job, but his work did not stop him from meditating or composing poetry. He soon began to gather followers around him, who would join him in the evenings to sing hymns.

Some people became jealous of his popularity. Rumors began to spread that Nanak was giving away free grain to the poor and squandering the funds. And when the rumors reached the governor's ears, he was forced to investigate. But nothing was amiss, and Nanak continued to work at the granary with dignity.

Kalu had a hard time believing that his son was usefully employed, so he sent Mardana to check on him. Nanak was

delighted to see his old friend again, and Mardana decided to remain there with him. In the evenings, when Nanak and his followers got together to sing, Mardana played the rebec.

When Nanak turned eighteen, he rented a separate house, and Nanaki set about finding a match for him. He was only nineteen when he married Sulakhani, a girl from a nearby town. Kalu came from Talwandi with a wedding party to celebrate his son's marriage. He gave his blessings, but he was also dismayed that Nanak had saved no money. He had given it all to charity.

In time Nanak's wife gave birth to two sons, Sri Chand and Lakhmi Das.

ENLIGHTENMENT

EVERY MORNING Nanak started his day with a bath in the river. One day he went to the river and did not return. Everyone thought that he had drowned.

The governor himself went to the banks of the river to see if his fishermen could retrieve Nanak's body, but the men found nothing. The whole town grieved, except Nanaki, who knew in her heart that her brother was unharmed.

During this time Nanak had a profound spiritual experience. The *Janam sakhis* describe it as a direct communion with God. He was chosen by God to spread his message, and he composed *Jap ji*, the first Sikh prayer, which contains the essence of Sikhism:

> *One being,*
> *truth is his name.*
> *Almighty creator,*
> *without fear,*
> *without enmity,*
> *timeless,*
> *never born,*
> *self-existent,*
> *the grace of the guru...*

After three days, Nanak reappeared, to everyone's astonishment. People wanted to know where he had been. But Nanak remained silent for three more days. Finally, he said the strangest words anyone had ever heard: "There is no Hindu; there is no Muslim."

In a society that was bitterly divided by the two faiths, a remark like this was not only unheard of, but dangerous. Some people dismissed it, saying that perhaps the river had affected his mind. But the Muslim rulers could not bear such an insult.

One Muslim official immediately sent for Nanak. The governor, who had more liberal views, begged him to dismiss the statement as something uttered by a holy man. But the enraged official challenged Nanak. If he saw no difference between the two faiths, he should accompany them for the *namaaz* (Muslim prayers). Nanak readily agreed.

During the prayers, the official noticed that Nanak did not kneel down and later asked him sternly, "Why didn't you join our prayers?"

"Whose prayers should I have joined?" asked Nanak. "You were only repeating empty words. Your mind was at home, worrying about the safety of the newborn foal. And as for the respected governor, his mind was busy thinking about the horses that he plans to buy in Kabul."

They both admitted that Nanak had spoken the truth and asked how they could become better Muslims. And Nanak replied,

> It's not easy to be called a Muslim.
> If he is, let him savor the religion of the Prophet as sweet,
> cast away his pride in worldly possessions,
> rid himself of the anxiety of life and death.

When he surrenders his ego and is merciful to all beings
he will be called a Muslim.

In 1496, when Nanak was twenty-seven, he felt the time had come to answer his divine call to take the message of equality to all of India, especially to the important places of Hindu and Muslim worship. The governor of Sultanpur begged him not to leave and offered him all his land and riches. But Nanak declined:

If there were palaces made of pearls
and they be inlaid with gems and jewels,
their plaster be scented with musk, saffron and
    sandalwood
the very sight of which would delight the senses —
even then may I not be tempted to look, to go astray
and forget to remember his name.

Nanak's wife was also sad to see him leave, and when her parents criticized him harshly for abandoning his family, Nanaki stepped in. She offered to take care of them, and being childless herself, adopted one of Nanak's sons.

NANAK'S TRAVELS

AFTER THE MONSOON, when nature was green and abundant, Nanak left home to brave the first of his four long spiritual journeys. His faithful friend Mardana went with him.

Nanak's first journey was to Assam in the east, the second to Ceylon (present-day Sri Lanka) in the south, the third all the way to Tibet in the north, and the last journey took him as far as Mecca in the west.

Nanak and Mardana covered short distances on foot or rode in bullock carts. But for longer journeys, they traveled with trading caravans. Joining a caravan was the only safe way to reach far-off places. The caravans were led by wealthy merchants of coral, spices, silver and embroidered silks. They were experienced travelers who used familiar routes and stopped frequently to rest at way stations. Donkeys and mules carried their goods, while horses, oxen or camels drew the wagons.

Nanak's mission took him to thriving cities and towns as well as little-known villages, temples, mosques, fairs and festivals. He and Mardana accepted the hospitality of humble homes and many times slept under the stars.

Nanak spoke with simple people as well as learned Hindu

and Muslim holy men. He converted kings and cured lepers. He enlightened stubborn priests, won over arrogant *pirs*, and even reformed thugs and cannibals, who fell at his feet, becoming his disciples.

Nanak used poetry, sermons and sometimes even gentle rebuking to spread his message of devotion to one God and, more important, the message of equality and compassion to all human beings regardless of their caste. He showed people that the promise of salvation lay not in renouncing the world but in embracing it — by living in a community and serving it.

THE FIRST JOURNEY

Saidpur

A T THE BEGINNING of his first journey, Nanak stopped
in Talwandi to see his parents. Kalu, now an aged man,
was sad to see his son in a *fakir*'s clothes and couldn't hide
his disappointment at the path Nanak had chosen. But his
mother was happy to have another chance to cook a meal for
him.

Traveling on foot from Talwandi, Nanak and Mardana
arrived in the small rural town of Saidpur. There they came
upon Lalo, a low-caste carpenter, sitting in the courtyard of
his mud house making wooden pegs. When Lalo saw the two
holy men, he hastily started washing a spot where they could
rest and eat.

Mardana didn't understand why Nanak had chosen the
poorest home in the entire town as opposed to one of the
many prosperous homes that could have welcomed them. The
food that came from Lalo's kitchen disappointed him even
more — thick flat bread made of coarse grain and a ball of
boiled spinach slapped on a worn-out copper plate. Nanak ate
heartily, while Mardana nibbled gingerly at his food.

Nanak accepted Lalo's invitation to stay longer, and news

spread in the town that a high-caste Hindu, traveling with a Muslim companion, was staying with a low-caste Hindu. People gossiped in hushed whispers and called Nanak a misguided man.

One day Bhago, a rich, powerful landlord, threw a feast to which he invited all the high-caste Hindus, well-to-do Muslims and holy men in the town. Everyone went, except Nanak. Sometime during the feast, Bhago found out that one holy man, new to the town, had not come.

"How dare a wandering mendicant refuse my invitation?" said Bhago, and he ordered his men to fetch the stubborn man.

When Nanak was brought to him, Bhago demanded an explanation.

"Is the food that low-caste host of yours serves better than mine?" he asked, pointing to the delicacies at his feast.

"I don't belong to any caste, and therefore I don't belong at your feast," said Nanak.

But Bhago insisted that Nanak accept his food too.

Nanak asked Mardana to fetch a piece of bread from Lalo's house. When Mardana returned, Nanak took the bread from Lalo's house in one hand and the bread from Bhago's feast in the other. He squeezed his hands. Milk trickled from Lalo's coarse bread and drops of blood oozed from Bhago's rich fried bread. No one was more surprised than Bhago himself.

"Why is there blood in my bread?" he asked, alarmed.

"Your bread is stolen from the poor, and Lalo's comes from honest labor," said Nanak.

Bhago fell at Nanak's feet and became his disciple.

Haridwar

AFTER A BRIEF VISIT to Delhi, Nanak and Mardana joined a group of pilgrims walking to the holy city of Haridwar. It is here that the sacred river Ganges, fed by glacial ice and melting snow, leaves the Himalayas, goes through the foothills and flows into the lower plains. To this day, Hindus go to Haridwar to wash away their sins.

Nanak sat on the steps leading to the riverbank, which were crowded with hundreds of men in white loincloths and women in colorful saris chanting mantras. As they bathed, they tossed handfuls of water toward the east, to their ancestors in the other world. Nanak watched the spectacle for some time and then stepped into the river and started offering water in the opposite direction.

"What are you doing?" shouted the offended worshippers.

When Nanak told them he was watering his field in Punjab, they thought he was insane.

"How can the water reach your field?" they asked.

"If it can reach your ancestors in the other world, surely it can reach my field," he said.

The jeering suddenly stopped, and the people gathered around Nanak, who gave a sermon asking them to question their empty acts of worship.

Gorakhmatta

FROM THE FOOTHILLS of the Himalayas, Nanak and Mardana trekked the rugged mountain paths of Garhwal, the mythical land of sacred rivers, gods and goddesses. They stopped in Gorakhmatta, where they stumbled into the territory of some yogis, who performed extreme forms of yoga. Most people dared not enter this place because they were afraid of the yogis' strange practices, magic spells and unpredictable tempers.

It was a cold wintry day. Mardana went to ask the yogis for some firewood, while Nanak waited under a shriveled-up tree. But the yogis turned Mardana away.

Suddenly the tree under which Nanak stood blossomed. The yogis came running over when they saw the miracle. They invited Nanak to join them so he could find his true religion and perhaps make them famous too.

Nanak asked Mardana to play the rebec and he sang,

Religion lies not in wearing saffron robes,
walking with sticks or smearing ashes on your body.
It lies not in shaving heads or blowing horns.
To live in purity amidst the worldly temptations
is the secret to religion.
Empty words do not make a religion.
It's not in fasting or going into trances
or traveling to foreign lands or bathing in holy rivers.
It lies in seeing all men as equal.

The yogis saluted Nanak and some of them became his disciples.

Traveling east from Gorakhmatta, Nanak and Mardana entered a forest dense with tropical trees, home to tigers, spotted deer, gibbons and monkeys. They soon lost their way, and their food supply ran out.

"I've had enough," complained Mardana. "You're a holy man. You don't need to eat or drink. But I'll die of hunger in these forsaken forests and won't live to tell the stories of our travels."

Nanak asked him to play the rebec to distract him.

"I have no strength to walk much less play the rebec. I must eat something right now or I can't go on," said Mardana.

Nanak looked around and found a soap nut tree, which bore wrinkly brown nuts. He told Mardana to eat the nuts to restore his energy, but he cautioned him not to save any.

Mardana ate the nuts, savoring their sweet, tangy taste. He secretly slipped some into his pocket, knowing very well that they might not find food for days. They continued their journey, and when he felt hungry he began to nibble on them again. No sooner had he taken the first bite than he fell down, clutching his stomach in pain.

"What happened?" asked Nanak, kneeling by his side.

"Stop my hunger or let me die," said Mardana, as he showed Nanak the fistful of forbidden nuts.

Nanak smiled at Mardana and threw the bitter nuts away. He took his companion by the hand and led him out of the forest to a village where they could find food.

But the endless traveling exhausted Mardana, and he began to feel homesick. He urged Nanak to return home.

After months of travel, they reached the outskirts of Talwandi. Nanak decided to stay in the forest, while Mardana went to see his family and then proceeded to Nanak's house.

Nanak's mother was overjoyed to see him and suspected that Nanak couldn't be far off. She grabbed some sweets and followed Mardana to the forest.

When Nanak saw his mother, he touched her feet with respect, and she kissed his forehead and cried with joy. Soon Nanak's father heard of his son's arrival, and he too went to greet him. Both parents begged him to return home.

But Nanak gently told them not to oppose his decision, as his mission was far from complete. After visiting Sultanpur to see his wife, sons and sister, Nanak set out with Mardana once again.

THE SECOND JOURNEY

Lahore

Nanak was determined to go as far south as the island of Ceylon. On their way he and Mardana stopped in Lahore, the bustling capital of Punjab, renowned for its splendid buildings, beautiful gardens and colorful bazaars.

There they met Duni Chand, a wealthy merchant, who was observing his father's death anniversary. He had fastened four flags to his roof, each representing a hundred thousand rupees, to show the wealth he had amassed.

Duni Chand invited Nanak and Mardana to join a symbolic feast in which he would offer food to the local Brahmins in honor of the dead. Nanak told him that there was no point in feeding a hundred Brahmins when his own father, reincarnated as a wolf, was lying hungry under a bush outside the city.

Duni Chand went quickly to find out if what Nanak said was true. Sure enough, he found a wolf cub lying under a bush, quivering with hunger and fever. He fed the cub and stayed there till it could walk away on its own.

This impressed him so much that he went straight to his

vaults and took stacks of rupees and placed them at Nanak's feet.

Nanak thought for a moment and then asked Mardana to take a sewing needle from his bag. He asked Duni Chand to keep it safe and return it to him in the next world.

Puzzled, Duni Chand accepted the needle but brought it back when his wife scolded him for being so foolish.

"How can I take a needle with me to the next world?" he asked.

"If a mere thing like a needle cannot go with you, how can all these riches that you are so proud of?" asked Nanak.

He then sang a hymn:

False emperors, false subjects, false the entire world.
False mansions, false palaces, false are those who
   dwell in them.

Nanak continued to say that everything was false except God. He believed that a person's deeds were the only true wealth, for they alone accompanied one to the next world.

Duni Chand became Nanak's follower and shared his wealth with many poor people.

Ceylon

HEADING FURTHER south, Nanak and Mardana traveled through countless towns and villages, preaching and talking with learned men of all faiths. Two years passed before they reached the sea.

They sailed to Ceylon, the fabled island of elephants, cinnamon and endless stretches of coconut palms. There they met the King of Jaffna, who asked Nanak to explain the mystery of existence. And in reply, Nanak sang,

Where do we go? Where did we come from?
Who gave us existence? Who will absorb us in the end?
How did we get ensnared? How will we unshackle?
With the sweetness of his name
in our hearts, on our lips,
easily we came, easily we'll depart.
Surrender to God will bring liberation.
The world is but a temporary home;
without his name, there is only emptiness
in the body and the mind.
Those who rejoice in truth
find him with ease,
says Nanak.
I would fall at the feet of such men.

As a result of his spiritual conversations with the king, Nanak composed many hymns. And the king and many of his subjects became Nanak's disciples.

In 1515, Nanak returned to Sultanpur. During his stay, he visited a tract of land between two rivers. He was captivated by what he saw — a freshwater lake surrounded by a forest, which was home to hundreds of migratory birds. The landowner was a disciple, and he pledged his land to Nanak. Here Nanak founded Kartarpur (city of God), a place where he would eventually spend the last years of his life.

THE THIRD JOURNEY

Tibet

WHEN NANAK and Mardana traveled to the north, they wore leather shoes and wrapped ropes around their heavy robes to keep warm. They joined a trading caravan bound for Kashmir and then proceeded to Tibet, passing through steep mountainous terrain before stopping at one of the highest lakes in the world. The landscape was breathtaking — the snow-capped Himalayan peaks surrounded a lush green valley.

The Buddhists living there presented a problem to Nanak, who they could see was a holy man. The lake, they said, remained frozen all year long, depriving them of much-needed water. Nanak hit the lake with his staff, and since then part of it has never frozen over.

Nanak had brought some rice wrapped in a banana leaf. The mountain people had never seen rice before. Nanak shared his food with them, but instead of eating it, they sprinkled the rice on their fields and buried the banana leaf. This place still produces crops of rice and wild bananas. Because of his miracles, the Buddhists refer to Nanak as *Rinpoche* Nanak, a term of respect for lamas, or teachers.

In the winter of 1518, Nanak made his way back to Sultanpur, where his family were waiting for him. During his stay, his beloved sister Nanaki fell ill and died.

Since there was nothing to keep him in Sultanpur, Nanak took his wife and two sons to Kartarpur. He established a commune there and left his wife in charge. Then Nanak set out on his last and most difficult journey.

THE FOURTH JOURNEY

Mecca

N ANAK WAS growing older and traveling was not so easy anymore. But he knew that without bringing his message to the Islamic world, his mission would not be complete. And so, accompanied once again by Mardana, Nanak set out for Mecca, the birthplace of Islam.

To make a journey to Mecca is called *hajj*, the ultimate pilgrimage for a Muslim. It is the holiest of places, forbidden to anyone who is not a follower of Islam. The ancient city of mosques and minarets was a remote place in a sandy valley surrounded by mountains near the Red Sea. The journey was rife with dangers — heat waves, scarce water, sandstorms and highway robberies.

Nanak and Mardana joined a trading caravan to cross the mountain passes into Afghanistan and then Iran. From a small port in the Persian Gulf, they joined a group of pilgrims and sailed for Mecca, disembarking at Jeddah.

Nanak met some Muslim holy men there. Wearing blue robes, a turban and a necklace of bones, and with a prayer rug tucked under his arm, he looked like a Muslim himself. But it was difficult to judge from his appearance alone.

"Are you a Hindu or a Muslim?" asked the holy men.

When Nanak told them he was a Hindu, they reprimanded him.

"Go back!" they said and hurried on.

But Nanak continued his journey, joining a pilgrim caravan with several hundred camels, and finally arrived in Mecca.

One day Nanak fell asleep in a mosque with his feet pointing toward the *mihrab* — a niche that shows the direction of the Ka'ba, the house of God. The mosque attendant was outraged.

"How dare you sleep with your feet in the direction of the Ka'ba?" he shouted, shaking Nanak.

"Forgive me," said Nanak. "Please drag my feet to whichever direction there is no God."

The irate attendant pulled Nanak's feet to the north and saw the *mihrab* move in that direction. He moved Nanak's feet to the east and the *mihrab* seemed to move the same way. And when he dragged Nanak's feet to the south, the *mihrab* moved once again. The holy men and pilgrims gathered around Nanak to find out how this could have happened.

Mardana played the rebec and Nanak sang a hymn in which he said that God was everywhere, in every direction. And the true God was within.

Everyone saluted him, saying that they had met a saint.

Saidpur

ON HIS WAY BACK to his family in Kartarpur, Nanak stopped in Saidpur to see Lalo, the carpenter. But Saidpur was in chaos.

Babur, the founder of the Mughal Empire, was making his third attempt to conquer India. The people of Saidpur tried to resist the attack and suffered the worst fury of the invaders. Babur's soldiers sacked the town, rampaging through the streets and markets, mercilessly slaughtering men and abducting women. The bloodshed reduced the town to an empty ruin.

Nanak and Mardana, like thousands of others, were taken prisoner. Nanak was so distressed by the massacre that for the first time he questioned God's will. The poetry that he composed in prison was intense and full of pain and protest:

> *Bringing the wedding party of sin from Kabul,*
> *Babur forcibly demands India as the wedding gift.*
> *The devil conducts the rituals;*
> *the bride's clothes are torn to shreds,*
> *her strings of pearls broken.*
> *Blood, not saffron, marks her forehead.*
> *For the sake of wealth, India is ruined and disgraced.*
> *When there was so much slaughter,*
> *so many cries,*
> *O Lord, did you not feel any pain?*

All the prisoners, including Nanak and Mardana, were expected to grind corn in hand mills. One day the guards were alarmed to see the hand mills spinning on their own, while the prisoners were busy listening to Nanak. They sent an urgent message to Babur, who regretted plundering a town full of such holy men.

"How can I make amends?" he pleaded with Nanak.

Nanak asked Babur to set the prisoners free and counseled him to be a just ruler and to show mercy.

The prisoners were released, and they returned to their homes to grieve their dead. There was mourning in every

house, and everyone remaining in the town became Nanak's disciple. But many, including Mardana, continued to be haunted by the massacre for a long time.

KARTARPUR

NANAK RETURNED from twenty-five years of traveling
to spend his last years in Kartarpur. He put away his
saintly robes and put on everyday clothes to practice what he
had been teaching. He resumed his own family life with his
wife and sons, and his parents joined them.

Nanak had spread his message of peace and equality far and
wide, and people from all faiths and castes flocked to listen to
his sermons. He continued to compose poetry, and Mardana
continued to provide music for Nanak's compositions, just
like he had on their journeys.

This is how *kirtan*, the congregational singing of hymns in
the early morning and late evening, became a Sikh tradition.
It was also in Kartarpur that the tradition of *langar* (a free
communal meal) and *sewa* (volunteering in the community)
started. In a country where the untouchables were shunned
and Hindus and Muslims never ate together, these traditions
were considered radical.

In 1535, Mardana, old and weary from their travels, fell
gravely ill. Mardana was a Muslim, but having become a Sikh,
the question arose as to how his body should be disposed of
after his death.

"Shall I make you a tomb?" offered Nanak.

Mardana declined. "When my soul has left its bodily tomb, then why shut it in another?"

Nanak smiled at his companion of more than forty years and said, "You are enlightened, Mardana. We will cast your body into the river."

In the early hours of the next morning, Mardana died. With a very heavy heart, Nanak lowered his body into the river and read prayers for his eternal peace.

Nanak counseled Mardana's family not to weep. There ought to be no grieving for a man who was returning to his heavenly abode, he said. Nanak then asked Mardana's son to take his father's place and play the rebec for him.

NANAK'S DEATH

NANAK WAS AWARE that his own end was drawing near, and he wanted to appoint a successor who would carry on his work. He had been closely watching one of his disciples named Lehna, who showed a deep understanding of his poetry and philosophy. He thought that Lehna would be worthy of the responsibility, but he wanted to test him one last time.

Nanak invited Lehna for a walk in the forest and then led him toward a corpse covered with a white sheet. He asked Lehna if he would join him in eating the dead body. Lehna obediently lifted the sheet only to find a dish of sacred food.

Nanak was so pleased with Lehna's devotion that he changed his name to Angad, which means "a part of my body." He placed five copper coins in front of Lehna and bowed, choosing him as the next guru.

The news spread that Nanak had chosen his successor, and that his death was near. Hindus, Muslims and Sikhs came from afar to pay their respects.

As Nanak lay dying, a dispute arose among the people. The Hindus said that they would cremate his body, and the Muslims insisted that they would bury it. Nanak himself settled the argument by asking them to put flowers on either

side of him — the Hindus on the right and the Muslims on the left.

"If the flowers on the right are still fresh in the morning, then the Hindus shall burn my body, and if the flowers on the left remain fresh, then the Muslims shall bury me," said Nanak. Then he asked everyone to recite the *Jap ji*. After this Nanak uttered Waheguru, the Punjabi word for God, then he covered himself and went to sleep.

In the morning, when his followers lifted the sheet, there was no body at all — only flowers, fresh and fragrant on both sides. The Hindus took their share and burned them, and the Muslims took theirs and buried them.

And thus in 1539, at the age of seventy, Nanak, guru of the Hindus and *pir* of the Muslims, died in Kartarpur, leaving behind a faith called Sikhism.

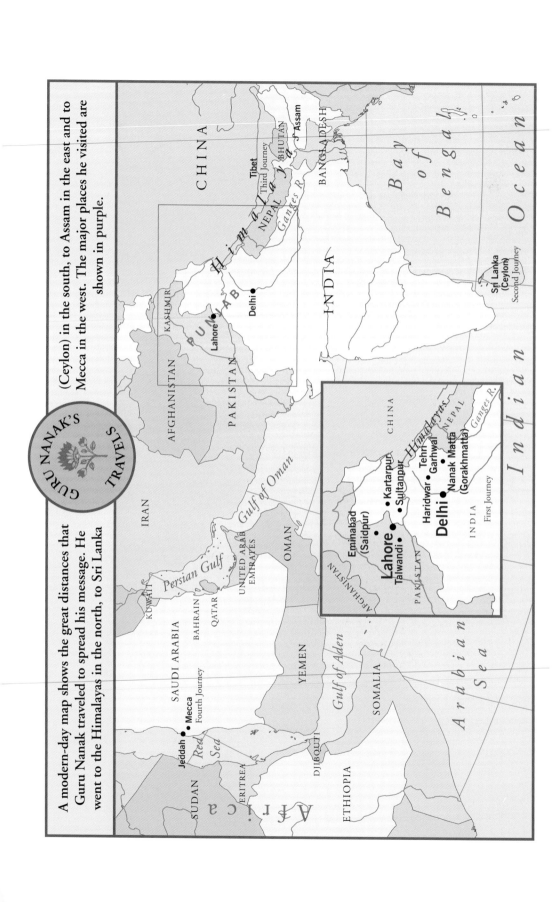

GURU NANAK'S TRAVELS

A modern-day map shows the great distances that Guru Nanak traveled to spread his message. He went to the Himalayas in the north, to Sri Lanka (Ceylon) in the south, to Assam in the east and to Mecca in the west. The major places he visited are shown in purple.

The Sikh Gurus

Guru Nanak (1469-1539) founded Sikhism. His birthday is now celebrated in November instead of April. It was changed in 1815 for practical reasons — once the harvest was over and the weather was cooler, there was good reason for peasants to celebrate. November also coincides with the time of Guru Nanak's enlightenment.

Guru Angad (1504-1552) recorded Guru Nanak's birth stories (*Janam sakhis*).

Guru Amardas (1479-1574) consolidated the tradition of *langar* (the communal meal).

Guru Ramdas (1534-1581) founded Amritsar, the holy city of the Sikhs.

Guru Arjan (1563-1606) built the Golden Temple in Amritsar and compiled the first edition of *Guru Granth Sahib* (the Sikh holy book). He was put in a cauldron of boiling water by the Mughals, becoming the first martyr in Sikh history.

Guru Hargobind (1595-1644) fought against the tyranny of the Mughals.

Guru Har Rai (1630-1661) built clinics for the poor.

Guru Harkrishen (1656-1664) was the child guru.

Guru Teg Bahadur (1621-1675) was beheaded in Delhi by the Mughals.

Guru Gobind Singh (1666-1708) made supreme sacrifices. He lost two sons in battle, and the other two were executed by the Mughals. He began the practice of Amrit (Sikh baptism) and created the order of the Khalsa (saint-soldiers).

Guru Granth Sahib, the holy book that Guru Gobind Singh proclaimed would rule the Sikhs.

GLOSSARY

Amrit: Sikh baptism.

Bhakti: Hindu spiritual movement in India in the fifteenth century.

Brahmin: Hindu of the priestly class.

fakir: Wandering religious devotee.

guru: Teacher.

gurdwara: Sikh place of worship.

Guru Granth Sahib: Sikh holy book.

hajj: Pilgrimage to Mecca, which every Muslim must make.

Janam sakhis: Birth stories that record the life of Guru Nanak.

janeu: Ceremonial thread worn by high-caste Hindu men.

Jap ji: First Sikh prayer, consisting of thirty-nine stanzas, which contains
the essence of Sikhism.

Ka'ba: Famous Muslim sanctuary in Mecca; the house of God.

kaccha: Long undergarment.

kangha: Wooden comb.

kara: Steel or iron bangle.

kes: Uncut hair.

Khalsa: Order of saint-soldiers.

kirpan: Small sword.

kirtan: Singing of hymns.

Kshatriya: Hindu of the ruler, warrior or landowner class. Guru Nanak
was born into this class.

langar: Free communal meal that is available to anyone who visits a
gurdwara.

mantra: Sacred sounds or words repeated in meditation.

mihrab: Niche showing the direction of the Ka'ba in Mecca.

Mirasi: Sect of musicians among Indian Muslims.

Mughals: Rulers of the Muslim dynasty founded by Babur, who was of
Turkish/Mongol descent.

namaaz: Muslim prayers.

pir: Muslim saint.

Punjabi: Language spoken in the province of Punjab, India.

rebec: Pear-shaped, three-stringed instrument, played with a bow.

Rinpoche: Term of respect for teachers.

rupee: Indian currency.

sewa: Volunteering in the community.

Shudra: Hindu of the untouchable class.

Sikh: Disciple, student.

Sufi: Muslim mystic; relating to Islamic mysticism.

Vaishya: Hindu of the merchant class.

Waheguru: Punjabi word for God.

yogi: Someone who performs extreme forms of yoga.

For Further Reading

The Facts about Sikhism by Alison Cooper. London: Hodder Wayland, 2007.

Guru Nanak by Eleanor Nesbitt and Gopinder Kaur. Calgary: Bayeux Arts, 1998.

I Am a Sikh by Paul Humphrey. London: Franklin Watts, 2008.

Religions of the World: Sikhism by Nancy Hoffman. Detroit: Lucent Books, 2006.

Sikh Stories by Anita Ganeri, illustrated by Rachael Phillips. Minneapolis: Picture Window Books, 2006.

Acknowledgments

I am deeply grateful to the following people who made the writing of this book possible: W.W. Macauliffe, whose translations of the Sikh scriptures and account of Guru Nanak's life were invaluable; the late Professor Harbans Singh, whose book on Guru Nanak truly inspired me (this book is a blessing he gave me on his death bed); Biji, my grandmother, who told me the stories of the gurus when I was a child; Professor I.J. Singh (New York University) for reading my manuscript and offering his support; Nan Froman, my amazing editor, who made the book what it is; and finally, my family, for their love and patience.

HARRIS COUNTY PUBLIC LIBRARY
HOUSTON, TEXAS